The Battle of Trafalgar

Panorama of History Series

This series has been created to provide a vivid portrayal of major events in world history. Each text is concise but authoritative, giving essential facts combined with an insight into the character of the period and people involved. Every book includes a large number of full colour illustrations and many more in black and white all researched from contemporary sources; these paintings, prints, maps and photographs all carry informative captions and are carefully integrated with the text. Published simultaneously with this volume is **Last of the Tsars**, and two more titles—**The Spanish Armada** and **The Industrial Revolution** will be published in April 1972. Further 'Panoramas' will be added to the series at regular intervals.

D0893006

Also available in the Panorama of History series

THE SPANISH ARMADA—Christopher Falkus

THE INDUSTRIAL REVOLUTION—Keith Dawson

LAST OF THE TSARS—Richard Tames

£1.50

The Battle of
Trafalgar

PAUL DAVIES

A Pan Original

PAN BOOKS LTD · LONDON

First published 1972 by Pan Books Ltd,
33 Tothill Street, London, SW1.

ISBN 0 330 02854 5

Made and Printed Offset Litho by
Cox & Wyman Ltd., London, Fakenham and Reading

Contents

Acknowledgements 6

I The Protagonists 7

II The Campaign 17

III September 14th – October 20th, 1805 . . . 23

IV The Battle 27

V October 22nd – December 24th, 1805 . . . 37

VI The Men 41

VII The Ships 47

VIII Aftermath 51

Appendices 57

Acknowledgements

There have been many books written about Nelson and the Battle of Trafalgar and this present volume is intended to be no more than a factual introduction to the subject. Those wishing to study the battle in greater depth are recommended particularly to read *Trafalgar* by Oliver Warner (B. T. Batsford Ltd, 1959, and Pan Books Ltd, 1966) and *Trafalgar: The Nelson Touch* by David Howarth (Wm. Collins, 1969, and Fontana Books, 1971). Other books to which I referred during the preparation of this work are: *Nelson's Battles* by Oliver Warner (B. T. Batsford Ltd, 1965); *Nelson* by Brian Tunstall (Gerald Duckworth Ltd, 1933); *The Battle of Trafalgar*, a collection of contemporary documents compiled and edited by John Langdon-Davies (Jonathan Cape Ltd, 1963, and Jackdaw Publications, 1966); *The Navy* by Oliver Warner (Penguin Books Ltd, 1968); and *The British Sailor*, A Social History of the Lower Deck by Peter Kemp (J. M. Dent & Sons Ltd, 1970).

The Author and Publishers wish to thank the following for permission to include the illustrations which appear in this book: The Carron Company of Scotland; *The Illustrated London News*; Musee de la Marine, Paris; National Maritime Museum, Greenwich; Radio Times Hulton Picture Library; and the Trustees of the Victoria and Albert Museum, London.

The Author wishes to thank John Scott Martin, the artist of the seven illustrations reproduced on pages 42, 43, 45 and 46; Patrick Leeson, who drew the maps; and Kyle Bewley Cathie and Cyril Hygate, both of whom gave valuable assistance in the preparation and production of this book.

CHAPTER ONE

The Protagonists

VICE ADMIRAL HORATIO NELSON, KB, was indisputably the greatest sailor of his and perhaps any other age. Born in the Norfolk village of Burnham Thorpe on September 29th, 1758, he was the fifth of eleven children (three of whom died in infancy) born to the Reverend Edmund Nelson and his wife Catherine, from whom he inherited important political and social connexions.

Educated in North Walsham and Norwich, he entered the Navy at the age of twelve under the patronage of his maternal uncle, Captain Maurice Suckling, RN, who was soon to become Comptroller of the Navy. He served on board the *Raisonable* until, in 1771, he was sent to the West Indies in a merchant ship commanded by one John Rathbone. He returned to England after twelve months to join the *Triumph* and then, in April 1773, he was chosen to accompany Captain Lutwidge in the *Carcass* on an expedition to the Arctic. He returned in October the same year and was sent to the East Indies in the *Seahorse*, but in 1776 he was invalided home to transfer to the *Worcester* as acting Lieutenant. Six months later he was confirmed in that rank and was appointed to the *Lowestoft*, a frigate commanded by Captain William Locker, and once again sailed for the West Indies.

In December 1778, Admiral Sir Peter Parker, the Commander-in-Chief, gave Nelson the command of the brigantine *Badger*, with orders to protect British trade in the Honduras from American privateers, and in June 1779, when he was not yet twenty-one, he was promoted Post-Captain in command of the frigate *Hinchingbrook*. Early in the New Year, he took part in the ill-fated San Juan expedition but he was recalled the day before the fort fell to take command of the *Janus*, then stationed in Jamaica. He was too ill with fever to do so, however, and for the second time in his career found himself invalided home to England.

He convalesced in the fashionable spa of Bath before travelling to London to join the *Albermarle* and in July 1782, he arrived in North America. From there he sailed with Admiral Hood to the West Indies and in May 1783, he was ordered home to go on half-pay for six months, a situation feared by every naval officer who was not of independent means. In March 1784, he was given command of the *Boreas*, bound for the West Indies where he became deeply involved in a prolonged trade dispute, earning praise from both the Admiralty and the Treasury for his exposure of illegal trade and frauds against the Government. It was at this time that he met and became engaged to Mrs Frances Nisbet, a young widow living at Nevis whom he married there on March 12th, 1787. (The bride was given in marriage by a brother

officer, Prince William, Duke of Clarence, later King William IV.)

Together they returned to England and Nelson went on half-pay for five long years, living with his wife and stepson at his father's home in Norfolk. In January 1793, on the outbreak of war with France, he was appointed to the 64-gun *Agamemnon* with orders to sail to the Mediterranean with Lord Hood. He was to remain there almost continuously for the next four years, losing the sight of his right eye in an attack against republicans in Corsica in July 1794, and being promoted Commodore in April 1796. Ten months later, he took part and distinguished himself in an action against the Spanish off Cape St Vincent for which he was made a Knight of the Bath, and that same month he was gazetted Rear-Admiral.

In July, Admiral the Earl St Vincent ordered him to attack the port of Santa Cruz in Tenerife, but he lost the advantage of surprise and the attack failed. During the course of it, however, he was struck in the right arm by a grapeshot and would have died had it not been for the prompt action of Josiah, his stepson, who was promoted Commander shortly after. Nelson was sent home in great pain, the amputation of his arm having been performed badly, and when finally he recovered it was due in no small measure to the nursing of his wife, Fanny. He was received by King George III and given an annual pension of £700; he earned the congratulations of the Admiralty and, in addition to the Order of the Bath which he was able to receive in person, was given the Freedom of the City of London. His one fear, as he wrote to St Vincent, was that 'a left-handed Admiral will never again be considered as useful', but it was a fear without foundation. Offered the command of the *Vanguard*, he gladly accepted and in April 1798, sailed to rejoin the Mediterranean Fleet.

His first task was to keep watch on the French in Toulon but he was blown off station in a gale and by the time he had refitted his damaged ship the enemy had sailed. Information provided by a neutral merchantman led him to believe that the French Fleet was heading for Egypt and he set off in pursuit, arriving in Alexandria

Captain Horatio Nelson, wearing Captain's full-dress uniform (1774–87). This portrait, which was started in 1776 and completed five years later, shows in the background one of the Spanish forts captured during the San Juan expedition of 1780. By John Francis Rigaud, R.A. (1742–1810)

The Battle of the Nile, August 1st, 1798, showing the start of the action at about 18.30 hours, with the French Fleet at anchor and the British Fleet rounding the head of the enemy line to attack. By Nicholas Pocock (1741–1821)

at the end of June. There was no sign of the enemy and he sailed to Syracuse to take on additional provisions before returning to Alexandria. And there, in Aboukir Bay, shortly after noon on August 1st, the French ships were sighted at anchor.

Nelson decided to engage the enemy immediately. Not only had he taken them by surprise, he realized too that the last thing they would expect would be a night action. He was right. His victory was resounding. Thirteen enemy ships were taken as prizes, and with a single blow he had put an end to French predominance in the area. He was greeted on his return to Naples as a 'Deliverer and Preserver', staying with the British Minister and his wife, Sir William and Emma, Lady Hamilton. Honours and rewards were heaped upon him. He was raised to the peerage as Baron Nelson of the Nile and Burnham Thorpe and awarded a pension of £2,000 per annum. The East India Company, the Czar of Russia, the Sultan of Turkey and the King of Naples all gave him expensive gifts and he received letters of praise from Admirals Howe, Hood and St Vincent, as well as from Prince William. And amidst all this, his love for Emma Hamilton grew to become his over-riding passion.

Within two weeks, however, the Neapolitan Army rose in rebellion and the King and Queen had to be evacuated. By the end of July, the Royal Family were reinstalled in Palermo and Nelson was created Duke of Bronte with estates worth an annual income of £3,000, but his infatuation with Emma was a source of concern to the Admiralty who in May 1800, accorded him permission to return home. 'I am quite clear,' wrote Lord Spencer in a private letter, 'and I believe I am joined in opinion by all your friends here, that you are more likely to recover your health and strength in England than in an inactive situation at a foreign Court, however pleasing the respect and gratitude shown to you for your services may be'. Spencer's letter was a model of tact but if it was written with the intention of preserving Nelson's marriage, it failed. Soon after his return and his promotion to Vice-Admiral, he and Fanny separated, and on January 29th,

Frances, Viscountess Nelson (1761–1831). As Frances Nisbet, a young widow living at Nevis, she married Nelson in 1787 when he was serving in the West Indies. The marriage was not a happy one and they separated in 1801. By an unknown artist

1801, Emma gave birth to a daughter whom they called Horatia. (A second child, 'little Emma', was born in February 1804, but she died five months later, in July.)

Nelson was now ordered to Yarmouth to join Admiral Sir Hyde Parker as second-in-command of an expedition to the Baltic, the purpose of which was to put an end to the Northern Convention of Russia, Sweden, Denmark and Prussia which had been formed to resist trade restrictions imposed by Britain. The Danish Fleet was attacked whilst at anchor in Copenhagen and the outcome was that Denmark agreed to abandon the armed neutrality. Nelson was elevated to Viscount and succeeded Parker as Commander-in Chief before returning to Yarmouth in July 1801, and within a few weeks, he was given the command of a defence flotilla drawn up to counter Napoleon's threat of invasion.

The Treaty of Amiens of 1802 brought peace to the country for the first time in eight years. Nelson had purchased an estate at Merton a few months before the Treaty was signed and moved there in October, sharing the Hamilton's household whenever he was in London, but in April 1803, on the death of Sir William, he and Emma were able to live openly together. The time they were to spend at Merton, however, was short. The peace was not of long duration and in May Nelson was given command of the Mediterranean Fleet, his task for the next two years being to watch the French Fleet and to engage it in action should such an opportunity ever arise.

When Villeneuve finally broke out of Toulon to embark on Napoleon's Grand Design, Nelson followed him across the Atlantic to the West Indies, returning to Europe to achieve, on October 21st, 1805, the objective which had been uppermost in his mind for more than two years. Soon after the start of the Battle of Trafalgar, Nelson was struck by a musket ball which entered the left shoulder to lodge in his spine. There was no hope of recovery. He died in the afternoon, in the hour of victory, and his body was brought back to England to lie in state at Greenwich. On January 9th, 1806, his remains were laid to rest in the crypt of St Paul's Cathedral in London.

The success of Trafalgar removed once and for all the threat of a French invasion. Only the death of the Commander-in-Chief himself overshadowed the glory of the occasion and it was a combination of these two things which gave birth to the Nelson legend.

Only forty-seven when he died, Nelson had spent more than twenty years of his life afloat. It cannot be denied that he owed the start of his career to his family and those he knew, but never once did he doubt his ability to reach the top and he did so through his own exertions and through learning from the lessons of experience. Nor did he ever forget his origin and his background. He was vain, he was particularly sensitive to criticism, he openly welcomed the honours and fame which his victories brought him, but his attitude to life was direct and uncomplicated. He knew exactly what he was fighting for and he fought above all for King, for Country and for Victory. He was possessed of a genius which only the sea could nourish; he looked after his men, he earned their love and devotion, and his success as a tactician lay in the 'Nelson touch', in devising a plan which was essentially new and simple but which, at the same time, was born from experience. It was this which singled him out from others and it was this which made him the greatest admiral of his day.

But it was not Nelson who was the architect of the Trafalgar campaign. ADMIRAL SIR CHARLES MIDDLETON was seventy-eight when he was called out of retirement to replace Viscount Melville as First Lord of the Admiralty. Born in Leith in October 1726, he had seen service in the West Indies before being appointed Comptroller of the Navy in 1778. He was made a baronet in 1781, elected Member of Parliament for Rochester in 1784, promoted Rear-Admiral in 1787, Vice-Admiral in 1793, and Admiral in 1795, and he was to be one of the Lords Commissioners of the Admiralty for two years before his retirement. Old though he was when William Pitt, the Prime Minister, summoned him to London, he accepted the task offered and was raised to the peerage as Baron Barham in May 1805. He it was who steered the two fleets to battle and it is to him as much as to Nelson that credit for the victory must go. When, in January 1806, he was permitted to retire for the second time in a long life, he returned to his house in the country to live out his days in peace and obscurity until his death in 1813.

Nelson's second-in-command at Trafalgar was VICE-ADMIRAL CUTHBERT COLLINGWOOD, a man he had first met in 1776 when

both were serving in the *Lowestoft*. Born in Newcastle-upon-Tyne in September, 1750, Collingwood joined the frigate *Shannon* as a volunteer at the age of eleven and saw service during the American War of Independence, being promoted Lieutenant in 1775. Two years later, he was tried by court martial for alleged disobedience and neglect of duty but he was acquitted on all counts and appointed Commander of the *Badger* on Nelson's promotion to post rank. He served at various times in the West Indies and took part in the Battle of the Glorious First of June in 1794 before being posted to the Mediterranean the following year. Promoted Rear-Admiral in 1799, he was given the command of the *Triumph* in the Channel Fleet and, early in 1805, a year after his promotion to Vice-Admiral, he was given command of a squadron to reinforce Nelson. He assumed command of the fleet after Nelson's death and was raised to the peerage as Baron Collingwood of Caldbourne and Hethpoole in Northumberland with an annual pension of £2,000.

But he was not as colourful a character as Nelson; experienced, courageous and distinguished though he was, he was thought to be aloof and reserved and something of a disciplinarian (and he was known to scatter acorns to his left and right whenever he went for a walk so that there would be a plentiful supply of oak trees from which to build ships). Nelson, however, had long ago broken through the mask and both loved and admired him. No two men could have been so dissimilar as they, yet each held the other in the highest respect: 'Lord Nelson is an incomparable man,' wrote Collingwood immediately he heard the news of Copenhagen; 'See how that noble fellow Collingwood takes his ship into action!' said Nelson as he saw his second-in-command lead the lee column into action at Trafalgar. But whatever criticisms might be levelled against Collingwood, a lack of conscientiousness was not one of them. He attained his rank without influence and remained in overall command for five years after Nelson's death, during which time his health was failing fast. Although he had been offered a command at Portsmouth, he

Cuthbert, First Baron Collingwood, Vice-Admiral of the Red, wearing Rear-Admiral's full-dress uniform (1795–1812). Collingwood first met Nelson in 1776. Appointed second-in-command at Trafalgar, he assumed overall command of the Fleet after Nelson's death. By Henry Howard (1769–1847)

delayed until it was too late: he died in March 1810, after seventeen years' continuous active service, homeward bound for England, and he was buried in the crypt of St Paul's at Nelson's side.

REAR-ADMIRAL THE EARL OF NORTHESK was third-in-command. The son of a sailor, he was born in Scotland and had served under Admiral Rodney, being several years older than Nelson, but he had no opportunity to distinguish himself in action. Neither Nelson nor Collingwood knew him well but there was no doubting his courage or his ability at Trafalgar: his flagship was the 100-gun *Britannia*, one of the oldest and slowest ships to take part in the battle, yet he took her into the thick of the fighting and sustained heavy casualties.

CAPTAIN THOMAS MASTERMAN HARDY was Nelson's Flag-Captain and had been appointed to the *Victory* in 1803. Born in April 1769, he had entered the Navy in 1781 and served under Nelson for several years prior to the Trafalgar campaign, commanding the *Mutine* at the Nile and serving as a volunteer in the *Elephant*, commanded by Captain Thomas Foley, at Copenhagen. He was made a baronet in February 1806, and appointed Commodore in the Portuguese Navy five years later. In 1815, he was made a Knight Commander of the Order of the Bath and promoted Commodore, and in 1819 he was given command of the South American station. Returning to England in 1824, he was promoted Rear-Admiral the following year and, exactly twenty-two years after Trafalgar, he struck his flag for the last time, joining the Admiralty as First Sea Lord under Sir James Graham. Appointed GCB in 1831 and Governor of Greenwich Hospital in 1834, he was promoted Vice-Admiral three years later and died at Greenwich in September, 1839.

Perhaps the greatest disadvantage under which both the French and Spanish Fleets laboured was that neither had won a naval battle within living memory. Of the two, the Spanish was probably the better, if only on account of the fact that their commanders had not suffered the political upheaval of the

Sir Thomas Masterman Hardy, Vice-Admiral of the Blue, wearing Rear-Admiral's full-dress uniform (1832–33). Hardy was appointed Nelson's Flag-Captain after the Battle of the Nile and served with him until his death in 1805. By Richard Evans (1784–1871)

Vice-Admiral Pierre Charles Jean Baptiste Silvestre Villeneuve (1763–1806), Commander-in-Chief of the Combined Franco-Spanish Fleet at the Battle of Trafalgar. From a contemporary engraving

Rear-Admiral Charles Magon, third-in-command (after Rear-Admiral Dumanoir le Pelley) of the French Fleet at Trafalgar. From an engraving by Maurin

French, and it was well known that Napoleon had little confidence in the ability of his admirals. The Emperor was a military man possessed of a first-rate military mind, but it did not extend to an understanding of the sea. He made the fatal mistake of underestimating his enemy and it was not to be wondered that his fleet lacked for morale.

VICE-ADMIRAL PIERRE VILLENEUVE succeeded Admiral M. La Touche-Treville to the command of the French Fleet in August 1804, but within a year he had lost the confidence of Napoleon, who had appointed Admiral Rosily to succeed him. Fate alone decreed that Villeneuve should still be in command at Trafalgar and it was at his feet, much to Rosily's relief, that blame for the Combined Fleet's defeat was laid.

Born of an aristocratic family in Provençal, he had been willing to serve the Revolutionary Government and had subsequently attained rapid promotion. A pupil of Admiral Suffren, the greatest tactician the French Navy has produced, he was several years younger than Nelson (whom he had first come up against in action at the Battle of the Nile) and had been promoted Rear-Admiral at the remarkably early age of thirty-three. Nonetheless, he lacked assurance and was unable to withstand the conflicting views of the Spanish.

His French second-in-command, REAR-ADMIRAL P. R. M. E. DUMANOIR LE PELLEY resembled him in many ways. Only thirty-five at the time of the battle, he too was a member of the aristocracy and although he had formerly served the King he had agreed to change his allegiance to Napoleon.

REAR-ADMIRAL CHARLES MAGON was third-in-command. Born in Brittany, he had considerably more experience than many of his fellow officers and was both courageous and impulsive with a sureness of character that Villeneuve certainly lacked. He had fought against Keppel off Ushant and Rodney in the West Indies, and had at one time been a prisoner of war in England.

Of the French captains, the best were undoubtedly Cosmao, Lucas, Infernet, Maistral, Gourrège and Baudoin; they were all men of experience yet their backgrounds were, in some instances, widely different—Gourrège, for example, had gained his command because of the Revolution; Maistral had gained his in spite of it.

ADMIRAL DON FEDERICO GRAVINA was the senior Spanish

commander and one of the most respected officers in the Spanish Navy. Aged forty-nine, he made no secret of the fact that he was serving under Villeneuve only with reluctance, and his war experience dated back to the Siege of Gibraltar. His second-in-command, VICE-ADMIRAL DON IGNATIUS MARIA D'ALAVA, was his senior in age by three years, and REAR-ADMIRAL DON HIDALGO CISNEROS, the next in line, had taken part in the Battle of Cape St Vincent, before Spain had changed sides to support the French cause.

But if the Spanish admirals had enjoyed less disruptive careers than their opposite numbers in the French Fleet, their experience afloat was less varied. Indeed, the experience of all the allied commanders hardly matched up to that of the British officers, and it was this, coupled with Napoleon's orders that battle was to be avoided if at all possible, and Villeneuve's inherent caution, that was to be a deciding factor in the conflict to come.

Captain Jean Jacques Etienne Lucas, Captain of the *Redoutable*, 74, the ship from which the shot that killed Nelson was fired. From an engraving by Maurin

Admiral Don Federico Gravina (1756–1806), the senior Spanish Admiral at Trafalgar who served under Villeneuve only with reluctance. From a contemporary engraving

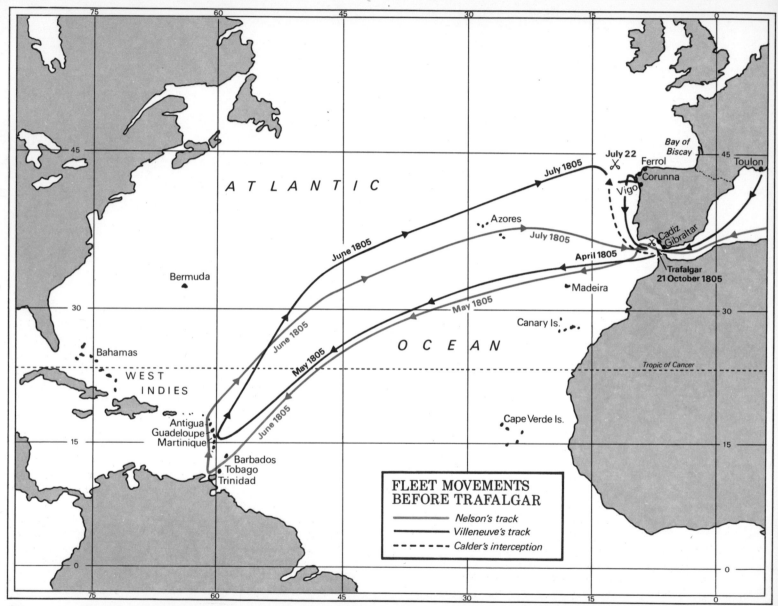

FLEET MOVEMENTS
BEFORE TRAFALGAR

— Nelson's track
— Villeneuve's track
- - - Calder's interception

ATLANTIC

OCEAN

July 22

July 1805

July 1805

June 1805

June 1805

May 1805

May 1805

April 1805

June 1805

June 1805

May 1805

Bay of
Biscay

Toulon

Ferrol
Corunna
Vigo

Cadiz
Gibraltar

Trafalgar
21 October 1805

Azores

Madeira

Canary Is.

Tropic of Cancer

Cape Verde Is.

Bermuda

Bahamas

WEST
INDIES

Antigua
Guadeloupe
Martinique

Barbados
Tobago
Trinidad

CHAPTER TWO

The Campaign

THE CAMPAIGN which culminated in the destruction of the Combined Franco Spanish Fleet at the Battle of Trafalgar on October 21st, 1805, began when, for the second time in his career, the Emperor Napoleon Bonaparte decided to mass an army along the French Channel coast in preparation for an invasion of England. Britain had been at war with France—apart from a brief respite following the Treaty of Amiens in 1802 —since 1793, and whilst Napoleon's forces had not enjoyed the success at sea which they had on land, it was essential for the Emperor to have naval superiority, in the Channel at least, before he could order the embarkation of his invasion army.

Napoleon well understood the difficulties and hazards involved in bringing his scheme not only to fruition but also to a successful conclusion without French supremacy afloat. 'To invade England without that supremacy,' he wrote in 1798, after he had returned to Paris from a visit to the Flemish coast, 'is the most daring and difficult task ever undertaken.'

He was determined to engage as high a proportion as possible of England's resources with the threat of invasion in order that he might be left relatively unhampered in his attempts to reach India. His eastern expedition of 1796 won him Egypt but the defeat of his fleet by Nelson at the Battle of the Nile two years later left his troops isolated and unable to progress further. England's foothold in the Mediterranean was confirmed and it was the retention of this foothold which was one of the underlying principles of British naval strategy at the time.

Undismayed, in the spring and summer of 1801, Napoleon began to assemble both ships and men at Boulogne to train for an invasion. Nelson, who had recently returned from the Baltic, was appointed to the command of a force stationed between Orfordness and Beachy Head with orders to destroy the enemy should he ever set sail from France. On August 15th, however, believing attack to be the best form of defence, Nelson attempted to capture the French ships as they lay at anchor in Boulogne harbour. He failed. The English assault was repulsed and the French Army remained where it was, only to be dispersed a year later with the signing of the Treaty of Amiens, by which time the Emperor had already started to turn his attention towards Central Europe.

The peace did not last for long. Exactly twelve months after the Treaty was drawn up, hostilities were renewed and English anger given full vent when Napoleon violated the code of war by placing every male Briton between the ages of eighteen and sixty who happened to be in France under detention.

Invasion was uppermost in his mind once again. The dockyards of France, Holland and northern Italy were ordered to start building barges immediately; the construction of the defensive mole to shelter the sea roads at Cherbourg was continued; troops were withdrawn from other frontiers and massed along the French coasts; and additional forces were held in reserve at Utrecht, St Omer, Montreuil, Ghent, Compiègne and St Malo.

England remained unimpressed. She started to prepare herself for the possible conflict to come, an intense hatred of the Emperor inflaming the populace. But coupled with optimism was the realization that so long as the French Navy remained undefeated at sea, the threat of invasion was always present. Provided England retained her naval superiority she had no reason to fear, but only with the French Fleet vanquished would the danger finally be removed.

The Admiralty responded to the concentration of Napoleon's forces in the traditional but effective manner. Numerous sloops and gun vessels were stationed opposite the invasion army, making it impossible for the French flotillas to gain any degree of success without the support of ships of the line. Admiral Lord Keith was given command of a small battle squadron, establishing his headquarters in the Downs, with a covering force provided by other bases at Great Yarmouth and the Nore, and a cruiser squadron, stationed in the Channel Islands under the command of Captain Sir James Saumarez, acted not only as a link between Keith and the Western Squadron (commanded by Admiral Cornwallis) of the main British Fleet, but also prevented any possibility of a break-out by the French from St Malo.

The Western Squadron was the centre of England's defence. Its duty was twofold: to exercise a close blockade of Brest; and to protect trade and safeguard the whole Channel position, of which the western approach was of vital importance.

Admiral Nelson was given command of the Mediterranean Fleet. He maintained a watch on Toulon for more than eighteen months, not once in all that time setting foot ashore, trying the endurance of his men to the limit and learning, before 1804 had drawn to a close, that Spain had reached an alliance with Napoleon, thereby increasing the French Fleet numerically by thirty-two ships of the line but not, in fact, strengthening it all that significantly in terms of performance.

Nevertheless, the Royal Navy formed a Spanish Squadron under the command of Admiral Sir John Orde with orders to patrol the area between Cape Finisterre in the north and Gibraltar in the south, keeping a particular watch on Cadiz. Nelson himself was far from happy at this new development. Although he had applied for, and been granted, leave on account of ill-health—and on this count alone the appointment was certainly reasonable—Orde was nonetheless the senior officer and the best placed to win prize money. Not only that, the creation of a Spanish Squadron divided Nelson's own command which had previously, and by tradition, extended to Cape St Vincent. But in spite of all this, because of Spain's entry into the war, and because he was a man who thrived on new problems and new dangers, Nelson decided to remain where he was.

It was just as well he did. On January 17th, 1805, Admiral Villeneuve escaped from Toulon.

The French put to sea with a total of eleven ships of the line and nine frigates. Their destination, although no one knew as such, was the West Indies, Napoleon preferring to put aside his invasion plans for the time being and concentrate instead on threatening British possessions in the Caribbean.

Nelson detailed two frigates to shadow the enemy, which they did until they reached the latitude of Ajaccio when they rendezvoused at the northerly tip of Sardinia. They reported that Villeneuve was standing south-south-west, confirming Nelson's belief that Napoleon was aiming at the subjugation of Italy. Immediately he took up a position to bar the French Fleet's way east, but a gale held him off southern Sardinia for several days, by which time other British frigates had reached the rendezvous.

Their lack of news convinced Nelson that either Villeneuve had returned to Toulon or he had taken advantage of the weather and swept round to threaten Greece and Egypt. Nelson chose the latter and sailed for Alexandria.

He was wrong. The French ships, manned by inexperienced sailors, laden with troops, unable to ride the heavy weather, had put back to Toulon. Napoleon informed Admiral Missiessy, who had escaped from Rochefort at the same time that Villeneuve had broken out of Toulon and who was now en route for the West Indies, that he was on his own and should act independently of Villeneuve.

The position was unchanged. The French Fleet, if not at large, remained undefeated and Nelson remained in control of the Mediterranean.

Napoleon now embarked on his Grand Design. Encouraged by Spain's apparent enthusiasm in her preparations for war, the Emperor issued a string of orders with the intention of uniting his fleets and bringing them to Europe so that they would be in a position to threaten the Channel. Admiral Missiessy, now in the Caribbean, was ordered to remain where he was and prepare to join other forces which would soon appear off Martinique. Similarly, Admiral Gourdon, stationed at Ferrol, was told to be ready to combine his ships with those of Admiral Ganteaume who, in turn, was to embark approximately 3,000 additional troops and, with a total force of twenty-nine, sail to Ferrol, scattering a blockading British squadron under Sir Robert Calder in the process.

From there, and with Gourdon in support, Ganteaume was to retrace his steps to Martinique, offloading 1,000 troops to strengthen the garrison before rendezvousing with Admirals Missiessy and Villeneuve and returning as hastily as possible to Ferrol. It was imperative that Ganteaume reached Boulogne and alternative arrangements, with the same object in mind, were made should Villeneuve fail to break out of the Mediterranean.

Villeneuve, assuming he had escaped from Toulon in the first instance and the Mediterranean in the second, was to relieve the Spanish ships under blockade in Cadiz prior to joining Ganteaume. Again, alternative orders were issued should the two fleets fail to meet, but in Villeneuve's case, no mention was made of Ferrol; instead he was to make for Cadiz.

Napoleon's ideas, whilst suitable enough on paper, were those of a soldier rather than a sailor: they ignored the winds and they assumed that the British would make no counter-move until faced with a numerically superior French Fleet. In fact, his Grand Design was a product born not only of an ignorance of

George Keith Elphinstone, Viscount Keith (1746–1823), Admiral of the Red. Keith was given command of a battle squadron which formed part of the defences drawn-up to counter Napoleon's threat of invasion in 1804. By George Saunders (1774–1846)

nautical affairs but also of small regard for the enemy afloat. Because he had successfully eluded Nelson once before, he trusted to luck in believing that his admirals could do so again. He was wrong.

News reached the Admiralty of hectic activity in all the blockaded ports and shortly after Sir Charles Cotton—who had replaced Admiral Cornwallis, who was on sick leave—had unsuccessfully tried enticing Ganteaume out of Brest, a British expeditionary force embarked from Portsmouth en route for Gibraltar and Malta, its objective being to prevent Sicily falling into the hands of the French. The convoy, under the command of Admiral Knight, put to sea on April 19th. Admiral Villeneuve, in the meantime, had managed to escape once more from Toulon.

Villeneuve had learned that Nelson was somewhere off Barcelona and had accordingly laid a course to the east of the Balearic Islands. The two British frigates following him felt certain that he would come near to the British Fleet in the Gulf of Palmas and they would have been right had not Villeneuve sighted a neutral merchantman who was able to inform him of Nelson's exact position. During that same night, he altered course to run inside the Balearics. The two shadowing frigates lost touch and the French ships succeeded in avoiding Nelson completely.

On April 7th Villeneuve sighted a Spanish squadron of six of the line under Captain Salcedo; the opportunity of accompanying the vessels to Cadiz was lost since Salcedo could not move without orders and Villeneuve dared not delay any longer for fear of being discovered. Two days later, on April 9th, the French ships entered the Atlantic.

Admiral Orde learned of Villeneuve's escape whilst he was provisioning and immediately fell back towards the Western Squadron. He lacked the force to risk involving himself in an action with the French, who had by now arrived off Cadiz. Straightway, the Spanish Admiral Gravina weighed anchor and before the British even had a chance to organize a watch, the Combined Franco-Spanish Fleet vanished into the blue.

To Napoleon, the news meant only one thing: there was now a real possibility of his invasion succeeding.

Meanwhile, in London, there was trouble of an altogether different nature. Lord Melville, the First Lord of the Admiralty, had

Admiral Sir Charles Middleton (1726–1813). Appointed First Lord of the Admiralty and raised to the peerage as Baron Barham in May 1805, it is to him, as architect of the Trafalgar campaign, as much as to Nelson, that credit for the victory must go.

been removed from office on account of a serious mishandling of Admiralty funds, and for a while, with the country threatened by war, the Admiralty itself was leaderless.

From retirement came Sir Charles Middleton, a man who had made his reputation as Comptroller of the Navy almost thirty years before. Although nearly eighty, Sir Charles agreed to fill the post during the crisis and, raised to the peerage as Baron Barham, immediately assumed control of the situation.

From Lord Mark Kerr, a captain who had been refitting at Gibraltar, word reached him that Villeneuve had succeeded in breaking out of the Mediterranean and joining his forces with the Spanish. At the same time, there was considerable anxiety for the safety of Admiral Knight's expeditionary force, for although no one knew exactly where Villeneuve was, the possibility existed that he might suddenly appear and threaten the convoy.

Nelson, however, had still not received notification that the convoy had sailed and remained where he was. When finally he learned of its existence, he discovered, too, that Villeneuve had managed to get away. He sailed for the Straits immediately and his dilemma on reaching Gibraltar was whether or not he should sail north to reinforce the Channel Fleet.

The convoy had put into the Tagus, much to the embarrassment of the Portuguese Government which was striving to maintain neutrality, and there was a report that Villeneuve had returned to Cadiz.

The report was, in fact, false, but it was not until May 10th that the convoy set forth once more. Nelson ordered the *Royal Sovereign* to reinforce Knight's escort and then embarked on his long chase of the Franco-Spanish Fleet.

But if there had been trouble in England, it was now the turn of the French to encounter difficulties.

Admiral Missiessy had reached the West Indies but had failed to link up with any of the other squadrons and, by the middle of May, was back in Rochefort. Only a week before his return, Villeneuve had arrived off Martinique. His first task was to achieve what Missiessy had failed to do. He attacked and eventually captured Diamond Rock, a small British outpost less than two miles from the French island from which a group of seamen, commanded by Commander Maurice, had continually and successfully raided enemy shipping, but the resistance he encountered enabled Nelson to make up for lost time and reduce the month's lead which Villeneuve had gained.

The French admiral, however, did not realize that he was being pursued. He laboured under the mistaken impression that Nelson was still in the Mediterranean and he received orders to remain in the area and threaten British interests. On June 7th, the day after Diamond Rock fell, Villeneuve was joined by two ships under the command of Rear-Admiral Magon. Nelson, now off Barbados, was told that the French had been sighted on a course which would take them towards Trinidad, and whilst he was disinclined to believe the information, he sailed south. Arriving to find no sign of the enemy, he returned north once again, soon learning that Villeneuve had moved north as well to appear off Guadeloupe. Nelson's presence in the area had done much to curb French aggression against British interests and he thought that, sooner rather than later, Villeneuve would return to Europe.

As the days passed and word reached Lord Barham in London of the developing situation, all indications pointed to a conflict off Cape Finisterre. Sir Robert Calder, then stationed off Ferrol, was reinforced and Cornwallis extended his fleet to the southwest. These moves, however, left Brest unguarded and Admiral Allemand lost no time in breaking out. Before Ganteaume could move likewise, Cornwallis was back on station and the French Fleet locked in port.

Meanwhile, Sir Robert Calder had confronted the combined Franco-Spanish squadron. The action fought was both confused and inconclusive, and whilst the English succeeded in taking two Spanish vessels, Calder himself received a reprimand: the clash had frustrated Barham's plans, leaving the enemy fleet still undivided and the crisis unchanged.

Nelson arrived off the coast of Spain ahead of Villeneuve and on July 20th he landed at Gibraltar. A month later, certain that the French were making for the Bay of Biscay, he anchored at Spithead. Fearing that the long months of frustration would bring him criticism, he was understandably gratified to find his reputation untarnished and his welcome as enthusiastic as ever.

On September 2nd, Captain Blackwood of the *Euryalus* drew

up at Merton, Nelson's country home, to inform him that Villeneuve had reached Ferrol where he commanded a fleet of thirty ships of the line. But by turning towards Cadiz rather than Brest, Villeneuve had also put an end to any immediate likelihood of invasion. Napoleon dispersed his invasion force and embarked on a land campaign.

Gradually each fleet was joined by further squadrons. Nelson began to prepare for the confrontation he wanted—an all-out conflict with the French. He accepted the command offered by the Government and, late in the evening of September 13th, he 'drove from dear, dear Merton, where I left all that I hold dear in this world', and travelled the road to Portsmouth.

The beginning of the end of the Trafalgar campaign had commenced.

Sir Robert Calder (1745–1815), Vice-Admiral of the Blue, wearing Rear-Admiral's undress uniform (1795–1812). Calder received a reprimand for his inconclusive action against the Combined Fleet in July 1805, an action which wrecked Barham's plans and which, if successful, could have made Trafalgar unnecessary. By Lemuel Francis Abbot (1760–1803)

CHAPTER THREE

September 14th-October 20th, 1805

NELSON ARRIVED in Portsmouth and set up his headquarters in the George Inn early in the morning of September 14th. Later that same day, he boarded the *Victory* at St Helens and, with the *Euryalus* accompanying him, made his way down the Channel.

He was off Portland on September 16th; on the 17th, off Plymouth, he was joined by the *Thunderer* and the *Ajax*, and six days after that he was approaching Cape Finisterre. In the evening of the 28th, he was with Collingwood and the fleet, and the enemy was visible in Cadiz. His long pursuit of Villeneuve was over.

Nelson had already formulated his plan of action. Explaining the scheme to Captain Keats of the *Superb*, he told him that he would form the fleet into three divisions in three lines. One, composed of about twelve of the fastest two-decked ships, would be stationed permanently to windward, ready to be ordered into battle when and if the need arose. The remaining divisions would be formed into two lines, and he would attack about one-third of the way down the enemy line from the leading ship.

In fact, when the time came, he was forced to modify the arrangement. His fleet was not as big as he had expected it to be and he eliminated the division that was to stand to windward. His ships would form into two columns, one under his command, the other under Admiral Collingwood.

'The Order of Sailing is to be the Order of Battle,' he wrote in his Fighting Memorandum.

'The Second in Command will . . . have the entire direction of his Line to make the attack upon the Enemy, and to follow up the blow until they are captured or destroyed.'

Nelson, however, realised that sea fights, like everything else, were subject to last-minute changes and he did not fail to take such a possibility into account. 'In case Signals can neither be seen or [sic] perfectly understood,' he added, 'no Captain can do very wrong if he places his ship alongside that of an Enemy.' It was a sentence which summed up the very essence of Nelson's naval tradition.

Meanwhile, the Combined Fleet of France and Spain was at anchor in Cadiz harbour, where it had arrived on August 21st. All was not going well. There was a shortage of food, a shortage of dockyard supplies, and not a great deal of respect between the two Navies, the Spanish adopting the view that the loss of two of their ships to Sir Robert Calder in July was something for which the French were culpable. The days passed. The situation hardly improved.

Sir Edward Berry (1768–1831), Rear-Admiral of the Blue, wearing Captain's undress uniform. Berry commanded the *Agamemnon*, 64, one of the last ships to join the Fleet before the battle. By John Singleton Copley (1737–1815)

At the close of September, Napoleon decided to order the Combined Fleet to Naples and then to Toulon. He did not believe that the enemy force off Cadiz was in any way substantial and he was convinced in his own mind that he had successfully managed to scatter the bulk of Nelson's ships by his Atlantic strategy.

Villeneuve himself, however, was far from happy. He knew he had lost the confidence of the Emperor (who had, in fact, appointed Admiral Rosily to replace him), and whilst as yet he was not wholly certain, he suspected that the recent additions to Collingwood's fleet included Nelson in the *Victory*.

On October 2nd, his suspicions were confirmed. Not only had Nelson arrived, his reports informed him that the British admiral already had several schemes in hand to bring about the destruction of the Franco-Spanish Fleet, one of which might easily be a repetition of the attack on French ships at anchor in Boulogne in 1801.

Five days later, in the evening of October 7th, Villeneuve gave the order to prepare to weigh anchor. Barely had he done so when it was countermanded: the wind was too strong and threatened to carry the fleet in the opposite direction to that which was intended.

Nelson now withdrew out of sight altogether, leaving only the watching frigates visible to the enemy. Villeneuve was in favour of sailing immediately. He outlined his orders to his commanders and found himself confronted with strong Spanish dissension. Admiral Gravina and his staff favoured delay: the British would soon be faced with a shortage of supplies, Gravina argued, besides which the latest batch of men to reach him were badly in need of further training. Tempers flared, remarks about Spanish courage were made—few of them complimentary—and for one moment it even looked as if a duel would be challenged.

A vote was eventually taken and Nelson's view that Councils of War invariably voted to do nothing seemed to be confirmed. The decision was to 'await the favourable opportunity . . . which may arise from bad weather that would drive the enemy from these waters, or from the necessity which he will experience of dividing his trade in the Mediterranean and the convoys that may be threatened by the Squadrons from Cartagena and from Toulon. . . .'

Reinforcements continued to reach Nelson. The *Defiance*, *Amphion*, *Naiad* and *Royal Sovereign* had all joined the British Fleet, and Rear-Admiral Louis, with five ships, had been dispatched to Gibraltar to take on provisions and to keep a general watch on the Straits.

The *Agamemnon*, under the command of Captain Sir Edward Berry, arrived on October 13th, and the appearance of the *Africa* the following day completed the Trafalgar fleet.

On October 18th, Admiral Villeneuve, still in command of the Combined Fleet (his successor being trapped in Madrid), unexpectedly ordered Admiral Magon in the *Algéciras* to sea. Accompanied by six other vessels, his task was to capture Blackwood's squadron, which was patrolling the area immediately around Cadiz, and to discover the extent of the force farther out to sea, but the news that Admiral Louis had reached Gibraltar made Villeneuve change his mind. He believed now that the British Fleet was as under-strength as it ever would be and he acted accordingly. The signal was passed for the fleet to be ready to weigh anchor.

The activity in Cadiz harbour, however, had not gone unnoticed. Captain William Prowse in the *Sirius* relayed the information to Nelson and at half past nine in the morning of October 19th, Nelson, by that time about fifty miles to the west of Cadiz, knew that the enemy was coming out. He ordered a general chase in a south-easterly direction and soon after signalled the fleet to prepare for battle.

Had Villeneuve succeeded in getting his ships out of harbour with the minimum of delay, he would have found the British scattered. As it was, however, the wind dropped, leaving Magon—who was first out—becalmed. Blackwood was able to dispatch a ship to warn Louis in Gibraltar and when, in the afternoon, the wind freshened again, Magon was unable to get back in. Villeneuve's hand was forced: the whole fleet had to sail.

By seven o'clock on Sunday morning, October 20th, the Franco-Spanish Fleet was clear of Cadiz harbour. Much of the day was spent manoeuvring backwards and forwards, each fleet jockeying for position against the other. Nelson was in no rush to clash with Villeneuve. He wanted the Combined Fleet as far away from Cadiz as possible, thereby preventing it from retreating to its port of refuge.

Sir Henry Blackwood (1770–1832), Vice-Admiral of the White, wearing Captain's full-dress uniform (1795–1812). Blackwood was Captain of the *Euryalus*, the ship to which Collingwood transferred his flag after the battle. By John Hoppner (1758–1810)

Just before dawn on the 21st, Nelson gave the order for the fleet to stand north by east, thus placing his ships nine miles to the windward of the enemy, and with daylight came the first sight of the Franco-Spanish Fleet at sea. 'We have only one great object in view,' Nelson had written to Collingwood twelve days before, 'that of annihilating our Enemies, and getting a glorious Peace for our Country.'

The time to fulfil that objective had now arrived.

The position of the two fleets at about noon on October 21st, 1805, shortly before the start of the battle

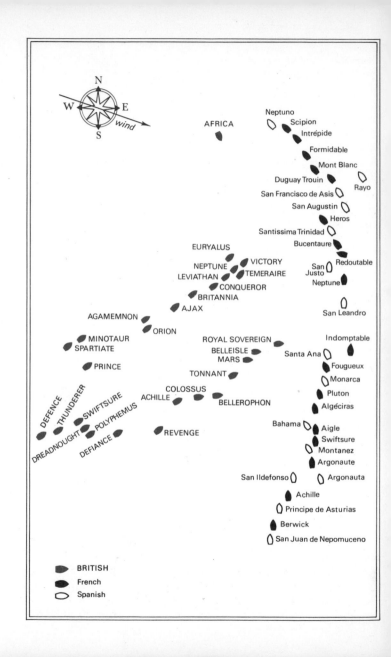

26

CHAPTER FOUR

The Battle

(Ships of the line of the British Fleet are set in bold capitals; those of the Combined Franco-Spanish Fleet are set in Roman capitals).

NELSON CAME up on deck soon after daylight on October 21st. Dressed in his customary frockcoat with the four stars of his Orders pinned to his left breast, he was in excellent spirits. Not only was he about to achieve his lifelong ambition—the defeat of an enemy fleet in open sea—he was supremely confident that victory would be his.

Already Villeneuve was manoeuvring as he had anticipated. The Combined Franco-Spanish Fleet had been heading south for the Straits until Nelson had ordered the British Fleet to divide and steer for the head and rear of the enemy line. Villeneuve, knowing that there were British ships provisioning at Gibraltar, could not commit himself to a southerly passage and he accordingly ordered his ships to reverse their course to the north and Cadiz.

Nelson signalled the fleet to prepare for battle. Throughout the morning, signals were made for the fleet to make more sail. Both Nelson in the **VICTORY** and Collingwood in the **ROYAL SOVEREIGN** were leading their respective columns and at eleven-forty, Nelson informed his second-in-command that he intended to pass through the enemy's line in order to prevent them from retreating into Cadiz. The tight formation of the Franco-Spanish ships, however, prevented him from doing so and the signal was followed by a second to 'Make all sail with safety to the masts'.

About fifteen minutes before midday, immediately before the order to close for action, the most famous signal in naval history broke out to the fleet: 'England expects that every man will do his duty'. (The signal was hoisted by Lieutenant John Pasco, who later recalled: 'His lordship came to me on the poop and about a quarter to noon said: "I wish to say to the Fleet, ENGLAND CONFIDES THAT EVERY MAN WILL DO HIS DUTY"; and he added: "You must be quick, for I have one more to make, which is for Close Action." I replied, "If your lordship will permit me to substitute expects for confides, the signal will soon be completed, because the word 'expects' is in the vocabulary, and 'confides' must be spelt." His lordship replied, in haste, and with seeming satisfaction: "That will do, Pasco, make it directly!" When it had been answered by a few ships in the Van, he ordered me to make the signal for Close Action, and to keep it up: accordingly, I hoisted No. 16 at the top-gallant mast-head, and there it remained until shot away.')

Soon after, the **ROYAL SOVEREIGN** came under fire.

The Battle of Trafalgar, October 21st, 1805: the beginning of the action, soon after midday, as the two British columns break the enemy line. The lee column is in the distance, and the weather column is in the foreground. By Nicholas Pocock (1741–1821)

Collingwood had been instructed to break through the enemy line at the twelfth ship from the rear but he moved up one in order to close against Vice-Admiral D'Alava's 112-gun flagship, the SANTA ANA. Immediately Captain Baudoin in the FOUGUEUX moved closer to the Spaniard's stern but the **ROYAL SOVEREIGN**, heading directly for her bowsprit, forced her to hold back to allow Collingwood through. Firing intermittently at the FOUGUEUX in order to create a smoke screen, the **ROYAL SOVEREIGN** ranged alongside the SANTA ANA to fire several broadsides, and within seconds the two ships were locked together.

Collingwood later described the enemy ship as a 'Spanish perfection . . . She towered over the **ROYAL SOVEREIGN** like a castle. No ship fired a shot at her but ourselves and you have no conception how completely she was ruined'. The fight lasted for more than two hours before D'Alava decided to strike his colours, by which time the **ROYAL SOVEREIGN** had suffered so heavily that Captain Blackwood in the **EURYALUS** was compelled to take her in tow.

But if Collingwood had captured the SANTA ANA, he was wrong in saying that no other ship had fired at her. Captain Hargood in the **BELLEISLE** had also left his mark. He had fired a broadside into her port side and another into the starboard of the FOUGUEUX before moving on to rake the INDOMPTABLE. Before he could do so, however, the FOUGUEUX reappeared and struck the **BELLEISLE**'s starboard gangway, allowing the INDOMPTABLE to fire across her bows before moving away, leaving the **BELLEISLE** and FOUGUEUX locked fiercely together.

The **MARS** was the third British ship to go into action and she suffered badly at the hands of the FOUGUEUX which was able to rake her, having dropped to leeward after the encounter with the **ROYAL SOVEREIGN**. The log records that 'At 1.15 Captain Duff was killed and the poop and Quarter Deck almost left destitute the Carnage was so great having every One of our Braces and Running Rigging shot away which made the Ship entirely ungovernable and was frequently raked by different Ships of the Enemy'.

One after the other, the ships in the lee column followed Collingwood's example and closed to engage the enemy. Nelson, meanwhile, had not been idle.

The **VICTORY** came under fire at about twelve-fifteen from Captain Remi Poulain in the HEROS, but it was not until some fifteen minutes later that she herself replied with her starboard guns. The French gunners aimed high, wishing to damage the **VICTORY**'s masts and sails in order to reduce her speed. It was during this opening onslaught that the British flagship's wheel was smashed and throughout the rest of the action she was steered by tiller from the gun-room.

Passing across the stern of the BUCENTAURE, she poured forth such concentrated fire that soon the French flagship was completely disabled. The **VICTORY** now came under fire from the NEPTUNE and then ran on board the REDOUTABLE. The two ships locked together and the **VICTORY** found herself tangled with the most deadly ship in the Combined Fleet.

Captain Jean Lucas had trained his crew to perfection. His aim in fighting was to board the enemy and his men were drilled with this objective in mind. At the start of the battle, he took up a position close to the stern of the BUCENTAURE and whilst he could not prevent the **VICTORY** from raking Villeneuve's flagship, he manoeuvred his vessel so that her poop was abeam of the **VICTORY**'s quarter deck. Grapnels were flung and the two ships fired broadside after broadside into each other; shot after shot rained down from the Frenchman's fighting-tops and for a moment it looked as if the **VICTORY** would be boarded, but the danger passed and the **TÉMÉRAIRE** came alongside the Frenchman to fire yet another broadside. A third ship came on her astern and, almost immediately after Lucas had rejected Captain Harvey's offer to strike, her main mast fell across the **TÉMÉRAIRE**, bringing down the latter ship's two topmasts.

'It would be difficult to describe the horrible carnage (aboard the REDOUTABLE),' wrote Lucas after the battle, 'in less than half an hour our ship was so riddled that she seemed to be no more than a mass of wreckage. All the stern was absolutely stove in, the rudder stock, the tiller, the two tiller-sweeps, the stem-post, the wing-transoms, the transom knees were in general shot to pieces.

'All the guns were shattered or dismounted by the shots, or from ships having run us aboard. An 18-pounder gun on the main deck and a 36-pounder carronade on the forecastle having burst, killed and wounded many of our people. The two sides of the ship, all the lids and bars of the ports were utterly cut to pieces. Four of our six pumps were shattered, as well as our ladders in general, in such sort that communications between the decks and the upper works was extremely difficult. All our decks were covered with dead, buried beneath the debris and the splinters from different parts of the ship. . . . He who has not seen the REDOUTABLE in this state can never have any conception of her destruction.'

Nevertheless, it was only when he was certain his ship would founder that Lucas struck his colours. The 74-gun REDOUTABLE had taken on two three-deckers and had immobilised the VICTORY. From her, too, had come the shot which killed Nelson.

Nelson had been pacing the quarter deck with Hardy when, about an hour after the flagship had first come under fire, he was struck by a musket ball which entered the left shoulder to lodge in the spine. He was carried below, covering his face with a handkerchief so that the crew would not realize who it was who had been hit, and William Beatty, the surgeon, was called to attend him. But Nelson knew that his wound was fatal. 'You can do nothing for me,' he told Beatty as he was laid upon a bed and his clothes removed to allow the surgeon to examine him, 'I have but a short time to live.' Beatty realized that he was right but he kept the news from the others until victory was assured. Everything possible was done for him; he conferred with Hardy, determined not to relinquish his command as long as he remained alive, but at half past four in the afternoon, Nelson breathed his last.

Throughout the time that Nelson lay wounded below deck, the battle continued as furiously as ever.

It was after two when the EURYALUS took the ROYAL SOVEREIGN in tow, by which time the BELLEISLE had broken away from the FOUGUEUX to engage the NEPTUNE. The fight lasted for almost an hour, ending only when the French ship was driven off by the arrival of Captain Redmill in the POLYTHE-MUS. Captain Hargood had taken his ship into the thick of the fighting, determined to carry out his orders and break through the enemy line, and it was to be wondered that the BELLEISLE was still in the action at all. She had received broadsides from the PLUTON, AIGLE, SAN JUSTO and SAN LEANDRO as well as the FOUGUEUX and NEPTUNE, and now she was to take on the ARGONAUTA, making the most of the advantage offered. The ARGONAUTA was already severely damaged and when finally she struck her colours, she did so to a ship almost equally battered—the BELLEISLE.

The BELLEISLE was the only British ship to be completely dismasted and, at the time the ARGONAUTA struck, she was on the point of being unable to fire any of her guns. An ensign was nailed to the stump of the mizzen mast and a Union Jack was flying at the top of a handpike; the SWIFTSURE, seeing the difficulties she was in, engaged the ACHILLE to spare her further broadsides, and one of the SWIFTSURE lieutenants commented later that 'Though an immovable log, she still kept up a smart fire upon the enemy whenever it was possible to bring a gun to bear'. Finally, the BELLEISLE was taken in tow by the NAIAD, as crippled as any other ship in either fleet.

The TONNANT, the fourth ship in the lee column to engage the enemy, came up against the MONARCA before tackling Rear-Admiral Magon's 74-gun ALGÉCIRAS. 'We went down in no order,' wrote Lieutenant Clements, 'but every man to take his bird. They cut us up a good deal, until we got our broadside on a Spanish ship in breaking the line, when we gave her such a thundering broadside that she did not return a gun for some minutes, and a very few afterwards.'

The Frenchman 'locked her bowsprit in our starboard main shrouds and attempted to board us, with the greater part of her officers and ships company. She had riflemen in her tops, who did great execution. Our poop was soon cleared, and our gallant captain shot through the thigh and carried below. During this time we were not idle. We gave it her most gloriously with the starboard and main deckers, and turned the forecastle gun, loaded with grape, on the gentleman who wished to give us a fraternal hug. The marines kept up a warm destructive fire on the boarders. Only one man made good his footing on our quarter-deck, when he was pinned through the calf of his right leg by

The Death of Nelson, October 21st, 1805. The scene in the cockpit of the *Victory*: Hardy is standing over Nelson and Dr Scott, the chaplain, is massaging his chest whilst Dr Beatty holds his wrist. By A. W. Devis (1763–1822)

one of the crew with his half-pike, while another was going to cut him down, which I prevented, and desired him to be taken to the cockpit.

'At length we had the satisfaction of seeing her three lower masts go by the board, as they had been shot through below the deck, and carrying with them all their sharpshooters, to look sharper in the next world; for as all our boats were shot through we could not save one of them. The crew were ordered . . . to board her. They cheered, and in a short time carried her. They found the gallant Admiral Magon killed at the foot of the poop ladder, and the captain dangerously wounded.'

The MONARCA now decided to rehoist her colours and straightway came under fire from the **BELLEROPHON**, which had previously engaged the AIGLE and was soon to engage the MONTANEZ, SWIFTSURE and BAHAMA. 'The AIGLE had twice attempted to board us,' wrote one of **BELLEROPHON**'s officers, 'and hove several grenades into our lower deck, which burst and wounded several of our people most dreadfully.

'She likewise set fire to our fore-chains. Our fire was so hot that we soon drove them from the lower deck, after which our people took the quoins out and elevated their guns, so as to tear her decks and sides to pieces. When she got clear of us she did not return a single shot while we raked her; her starboard side was entirely beaten in . . .'

Close astern of the **BELLEROPHON** came the **COLOSSUS** and the **ACHILLE**, the latter ship engaging two others before locking with the BERWICK, which eventually surrendered to her. The SWIFTSURE and BAHAMA both struck to the **COLOSSUS**.

The 74-gun **REVENGE** out-sailed the **DREADNOUGHT** and the **POLYTHEMUS** to open fire on the SAN ILDEFONSO. Captain Moorsom also dismasted the ACHILLE before engaging Admiral Gravina's flagship, the 112-gun PRINCIPE DE ASTURIAS. The Spanish ship, according to one of the men aboard the **REVENGE**, 'ran her bowsprit over our poop, with a number of her crew on it, and in her fore-rigging. Two or three hundred men were ready to follow, but they caught a Tartar, for their design was discovered, and our marines with their small-arms, and the carronades on the poop, loaded with canister shot, swept them off so fast that they were glad to sheer off.'

Captain Durham in the **DEFIANCE** ran alongside the AIGLE and sent a boarding party to take possession of the quarter deck and poop. Within a matter of minutes, the French colours had been replaced by those of the English, but as the fighting continued as fiercely as ever, the boarders were recalled, the ship cast off and broadside fire resumed. It was only a question of time before the AIGLE called for quarter, however; she was already seriously damaged and her casualties were high, and half an hour later, a second boarding party from the **DEFIANCE** had taken possession of her.

It was now the turn of the **DREADNOUGHT** to go into action. She came alongside the Spanish Captain Churruca's SAN JUAN DE NEPOMUCENO, which struck her colours within ten minutes, and next turned her attention to Gravina's flagship, already heading towards Cadiz.

The remaining ships in Collingwood's line suffered only light casualties, and the situation repeated itself in the weather column. Again, it was the leading ships which saw most of the action.

'It was a beautiful sight,' wrote Midshipman Badcock of the **NEPTUNE**, describing the appearance of the Combined Fleet as Nelson's column approached, 'when their line was completed, their broadsides turned towards us, showing their iron teeth, and now and then trying the range of a shot to ascertain the distance, that they might, the moment we came within point blank (about six hundred yards), open their fire upon our van ships . . .

'Some of the enemy's ships were painted like ourselves, with yellow sides, some with a broad single red or yellow streak, others all black, and the noble SANTISSIMA TRINIDAD, with four distinct lines of red, with a white ribbon between them, made her seem a superb man-of-war, which indeed she was. Her appearance was imposing, her head splendidly ornamented with a colossal group of figures, painted white, representing the Holy Trinity, from which she took her name.'

The **NEPTUNE** was the third British ship in the weather

The Battle of Trafalgar, October 21st, 1805. By Clarkson Stanfield

column, after the **VICTORY** and the **TÉMÉRAIRE**, to go into action. Andrew Green, the signal officer, recalled that 'The **VICTORY** open'd her fire and endeavoured to pass under Stern of the French Admiral in the **BUCENTAURE**. The **REDOUTABLE** closed so near, to support his Commander in Chief, that the **VICTORY** was obliged to lay that ship on board, when both ships paid off before the wind.

'The **TÉMÉRAIRE**, in following gallantly Lord Nelson's ship, fell on the opposite side of the **REDOUTABLE**, from the same cause, and the **INTRÉPIDE** alongside the **TÉMÉRAIRE**: The four ships lock'd in and on board each other, and their Sterns to us. We put the ship's helm a Starboard and the **NEPTUNE** passed between the **VICTORY** and **BUCENTAURE**, with which ship we were warmly engaged (the **CONQUEROR**'s Jib-boom touching our Taffrail). We passed on to the **SANTISSIMA TRINIDAD**, whose Stern was entirely exposed to our fire without being able to return a single shot with effect. At 50 minutes past one observed her Main and Mizen Masts fall overboard, gave three cheers, she then paid off and brought us nearly on her lee Beam, in about a quarter of an hour more, her Foremast fell over her Stern, and shortly after an Officer threw a Union Jack over her Starboard Quarter, hailed the **NEPTUNE** and said they had struck. The Van of the Enemy now wore and were crossing us apparently with an intent to support their Admirals. The **CONQUEROR** at this time passed over to windward to engage them. Put our helm a port and fired successfully with six sail of the line that passed to windward, the remaining three going to leeward. Observed the **LEVIATHAN** and another ship closely engaged with two of the Enemy's ships who had bore up and soon after struck.'

The **LEVIATHAN** was in fact engaged with the ŞAN AUGUSTIN, which she carried by boarding. The **CONQUEROR** engaged the BUCENTAURE and the SANTISSIMA TRINIDAD, and the INTRÉPIDE struck to Captain Codrington in the **ORION**.

Meanwhile, however, a number of French ships, including Rear-Admiral Dumanoir le Pelley in the FORMIDABLE, were so far ahead that they were unable to take part in the battle.

Captain Digby in the 64-gun **AFRICA** was far to the north of the main British column but he went into action soon after the **ROYAL SOVEREIGN**, engaging Commodore Valdez in the NEPTUNO before going to the assistance of the **NEPTUNE**, which was engaged with the SANTISSIMA TRINIDAD.

It was three o'clock in the afternoon when Dumanoir le Pelley was able to bring his ships about, by which time the worst was over. But the French admiral decided to make for the rear where the PRINCIPE DE ASTURIAS was under heavy fire.

Two ships only in Nelson's division had not yet been in action, the **SPARTIATE** and the **MINOTAUR**, and they soon realized that the FORMIDABLE was intent on cutting them off. They held their course across the bows of the French ship, raking her as they passed before heaving to between her and the **VICTORY**, where they remained to force the enemy vessels to keep their wind.

The BUCENTAURE now struck and Collingwood signalled for ships to come to wind to hold off the FORMIDABLE which threatened to assist the PRINCIPE DE ASTURIAS. The French admiral, realizing that all was lost, turned away and sailed for the Straits of Gibraltar.

When word reached Admiral Collingwood that Nelson had been wounded and was dying, victory had been won. Admiral Villeneuve was a captive and his fleet was scattered. Four ships had sailed to the south with Dumanoir le Pelley and of the eighteen remaining in the battle area, the ACHILLE was on fire and was soon to sink and thirteen were already manned by prize crews. Seventeen were dismasted.

The destruction of the Combined Franco-Spanish Fleet confirmed England's superiority afloat. It had taken more than two years to bring the French ships to action and now that they had been vanquished, any possibility of Napoleon ordering an invasion was out of the question. Although another ten years were to pass before the French Emperor was finally defeated at Waterloo, Nelson's victory at the Battle of Trafalgar foiled for ever his hopes of subjugating England through invasion.

The Battle of Trafalgar, October 21st, 1805: the end of the action, at about 17.30 hours. In the foreground, the battered British ships lie with their prizes whilst beyond, ten enemy ships make their escape. By Nicholas Pocock (1741–1821)

Horatio, Viscount Nelson, Vice-Admiral of the White, a portrait painted at Greenwich Hospital in the winter of 1797–98, when Nelson was recovering from the loss of his arm. By Lemuel Francis Abbot (1760–1803)

CHAPTER FIVE

October 22nd-December 24th, 1805

WITH NIGHTFALL came added complications. It was apparent that the damage inflicted on some of the ships was so great that they were barely able to keep afloat, and on board those which hadn't been able to put into the safety of Cadiz, all hands were occupied with repairs, with looking after the wounded, disposing of the dead, and manning the pumps.

Nelson had been correct when he had said that morning that a storm was blowing up. Throughout the night, the wind increased to gale force and remained so for several days. Some captains remembered his orders to anchor and some did so. Others, however, could not. Anchors and cables alike suffered as much damage as other parts of the ships and there were some who felt that the more sea-room they had, the better it would be.

The British crews were reduced, too, through the necessity of manning the prizes. Enemy casualties were considerable and the first task facing the prize crews was to heave bodies overboard before securing the prisoners. The **MINOTAUR** took the NEPTUNO in tow until the hawser broke, and the SAN JUAN DE NEPOMUCENO, although she had struck to the **DREAD-NOUGHT**, was manned by a crew from the **TONNANT**.

The ALGÉCIRAS, now commanded by Lieutenant Bennett of the **TONNANT**, drifted too close to the shore and the crew,

numbering no more than fifty, was unable to attend to the rigging as well as to guard the 270 prisoners. Bennett had no alternative but to release them, whereupon the French announced that they had retaken possession of the ship, nevertheless promising to release the English if they assisted in taking the vessel to Cadiz.

The wind continued throughout the 22nd, blowing from the south which made it difficult for the British to take their prizes to Gibraltar.

That afternoon, Captain Cosmao in the PLUTON, together with the INDOMPTABLE, NEPTUNE, RAYO and SAN FRANCISCO DE ASIS, all of which had made the safety of Cadiz, decided to venture out of the harbour in the hope of rescuing some of the prizes still in difficulties in the bay.

He had one success. The **THUNDERER** had time to withdraw her prize crew from the SANTA ANA before she was retaken, but Collingwood quickly called up support to thwart Cosmao's intention. Nor was luck with the Spaniard in any other form: he lost three of the vessels accompanying him, the INDOMPTABLE and SAN FRANCISCO DE ASIS being driven ashore and the RAYO losing her masts before surrendering to a disappointed but

surprised Captain Sir Pulteney Malcolm in the **DONEGAL**, too recently out of Gibraltar to have taken part in the battle.

But if Cosmao failed to retake the prizes, the weather determined that they would not reach Gibraltar. The REDOUTABLE sank, and the BUCENTAURE, BERWICK, FOUGUEUX and AIGLE were all wrecked. Only four reached port—the SWIFT-SURE, BAHAMA, SAN JUAN DE NEPOMUCENO and SAN ILDEFONSO.

Now that Collingwood had succeeded Nelson to the overall command, the admiral was determined that no loose ends should be left undone. He was under the impression that Admiral Dumanoir le Pelley, whom he had last seen trying to be of assistance to the PRINCIPE DE ASTURIAS, had gone about and put into Cadiz, and knowing as he did that the Frenchman, in comparison to some of the ships, was relatively undamaged, Collingwood maintained a watch on the port until he was certain the FORMIDABLE was not there. At the same time, Admiral Allemand was also at large so the danger existed that the British Fleet would come under attack from the west.

In the event it was neither Collingwood nor any of the other captains who had taken part in the battle who encountered Dumanoir le Pelley. The French admiral, although he had headed for the Straits, had not passed through them, and when the storm struck, his squadron was unable to stand against it. Late in the evening of the 22nd, he sighted what he took to be the ships of Rear-Admiral Louis and decided to back off to the west in the hope of joining Allemand.

Sir Richard Strachan, Capturing part of the Trafalgar Fleet. Realizing that the battle was lost, Rear-Admiral Dumanoir le Pelley headed north towards Ferrol; some ten days later, he was sighted and compelled to engage Sir Richard Strachan's squadron in action

On the 25th, the squadron turned to the north and, four days later, was off Cape St Vincent. Allemand continued to elude him and he determined to head on to Rochefort, as unaware that Sir Richard Strachan was ahead of him as was the British captain of Dumanoir le Pelley's presence.

The French ships were forced to keep near the coast and, although they passed Finisterre without being sighted, they did not escape the notice of Captain Baker in the PHOENIX. Baker had heard—wrongly as it transpired—that Allemand was in the Bay of Biscay, and was now making for a rendezvous with Strachan. Dumanoir le Pelley detached the DUGUAY-TROUIN to cut him off, but Baker successfully reached the CAESAR to report that he had been pursued by Allemand.

Strachan sighted the French ships during the night of November 2nd-3rd and although Dumanoir le Pelley altered course to mislead him, Strachan was convinced that the enemy was making for Ferrol.

The CAESAR by this time had been joined by the HERO, COURAGEUX and Captain Lord William Fitzroy's frigate, the AEOLUS, and at dawn on the 3rd, with the arrival of the SANTA MARGARITA, PHOENIX, NAMUR and REVOLUTIONAIRE, the squadron was complete. The chase continued all day and night; Dumanoir le Pelley, unable to make Ferrol, was now heading for Rochefort, but the British ships were slowly overhauling him and, soon after daybreak on November 4th, he hauled to wind in line of battle to engage the enemy.

Strachan signalled his captains that he intended to attack the French line at its centre and rear and, leading in the CAESAR, he manoeuvred himself against Dumanoir le Pelley's flagship. The British frigates stood to leeward to engage Captain Berenger in the SCIPION as the other ships went into action, but the outcome was a foregone conclusion. 'The French squadron fought to admiration,' Strachan wrote later, but superiority was his. It was only when Dumanoir le Pelley arrived on board the **CAESAR**, however, that Strachan realized who it was he had been fighting. He learned, too, for the first time, the outcome of the Battle of Trafalgar.

With Dumanoir le Pelley out of the action, the campaign as such was over. Allemand, however, was still at large having provisioned at the Spanish garrison in the Canary Islands, but it was not until the middle of December that he knew for certain that the Combined Franco-Spanish Fleet had been destroyed. He was off the coast of Portugal at the time, having spent his weeks afloat preying on British merchantmen, and he learned that a large body of ships was on the lookout for him.

The weather favoured him and he succeeded in avoiding capture. On December 24th, 1805, more than two months after the battle, Admiral Allemand finally reached Rochefort, one of the few survirors of his Emperor's Grand Design.

CHAPTER SIX

The Men

'WHATEVER MAY be said about this boasted land of liberty, whenever a youth resorts to a receiving ship for shelter and hospitality, he from that moment must take leave of the liberty to speak or act; he may think but he must confine his thoughts to the hold of his mind and never suffer them to escape through the hatchway of utterance.'

So wrote the pseudonymous Jack Nastyface, describing conditions in the Navy at the time of the Napoleonic War. There is no doubt that his assertions were correct, but he was living in an age when the treatment and conditions of sailors on board His Majesty's ships were gradually being improved.

During the period of peace between the end of the American War of Independence and the start of the war against Napoleon, the Navy was commanded by men intent on maintaining its efficiency and standing. Admiral Lord Howe and the Earl of Chatham, as successive First Lords of the Admiralty, were determined not to allow the fleet to suffer from neglect or inefficiency and corruption, as had been the case at the close of the Seven Years' War, but when hostilities were resumed in 1793, Lord Chatham was nonetheless faced with the problem of bringing the Navy up to its full complement of men.

The number of sailors and marines voted by Parliament in its annual Estimate for 1792 was only 16,000—a number hopelessly inadequate for a fleet which was rapidly being expanded. (Nine years later, in 1801, this figure had risen to 135,000.) The measures taken to increase the strength of the fleet were inevitably reflected in the character of the British sailor himself, yet there is no doubt that throughout the Napoleonic War he was never once surpassed either in courage and skill or discipline.

As an incentive for a man to sign on voluntarily, he was given a bounty of thirty shillings in addition to the money he received as his standard pay. This sum, however, was supplemented by additional bounties offered by the various port authorities: in 1794, for example, the Lord Mayor of London proposed that able seamen should receive ten guineas and, by 1795, several seaport towns were offering as much as thirty pounds.

The bounty system worked up to a point but it also left a great deal to be desired in other ways. The number of volunteers recruited was by no means sufficient and a sizeable percentage of them were the misfits of civilian life, enticed to join by the promise of bounty and with every intention of deserting at the first opportunity. (Some even signed on a second time, under a different name, so that they might qualify for a second bounty.)

The Marine Society, founded by Jonas Hanway in 1756, pro-

Vice-Admiral in full-dress uniform, 1805

Flag-Captain in full-dress uniform, 1805

Lieutenant in undress uniform, 1805

Midshipman, 1805

vided two classes of recruit: men who joined ships as landmen who were paid sixteen shillings a month until they were skilled enough to be rated ordinary seamen; and boys, one group aged between thirteen and fifteen who became servants for officers at £4 per annum, and another aged between fifteen and seventeen who received an annual wage of £5 until they, too, became ordinary seamen.

The pressgangs continued to be active, both on shore and at sea, although the men they pressed tended to be of the worst possible type. Merchant ships were often ordered to heave to and a naval recruiting party went aboard to press many of the best seamen whilst leaving behind a number of its own trouble-makers. It mattered not what nationality a man was, be he Irish or American, black or white, and there was even a Frenchman serving on board the *Victory* at the time of Trafalgar.

The Quota Act of 1795 called for each county to provide a certain number of men in proportion to its population for naval service. Yorkshire, for example, was required to supply 1,081 and Rutland 27, and in April the same year, the Act was extended to the seaport towns. London had to provide 5,704 men and Newcastle 1,240. Over 30,000 sailors joined the fleet in this way and they were known on board as Lord Mayor's Men since many of them had been hauled from prison in order to satisfy the quota. Scorned as scum unworthy of serving side by side with qualified seamen, they were regarded as objects of derision rather than pity and invariably led a wretched existence. The fact that more often than not they received a larger bounty than that paid to the volunteer only served to exacerbate the situation, and it was undoubtedly they who gave the Navy its bad name. The local authorities, forced to fill the quota, were understandably anxious to be rid of their town's less desirable elements for as long a period as possible and it was exactly that sort of character they selected. A criminal on land, he was the cause of much of the resentment on the lower deck and it was he who was essentially responsible for the increase in flogging. Indeed, Captain Edward Brenton, writing in his *Naval History of Great Britain*, said that 'we conceive [the quota bounty] to have been the most ill-advised and fatal measure ever adopted by the Government for manning the fleet. The seamen who voluntarily enlisted in 1793, and fought some of the most glorious of our battles, received the comparatively small bounty of £5. These brave fellows saw men, totally ignorant of the profession, the very refuse and outcasts of society, fleeing from justice and the vengeance of the law, come on board with bounty to the amount of £70.'

Once he had left the receiving ship, however, conditions improved. Each sailor messed in a space between two guns and, restricted though this was, there was room enough for his hammock, his few items of furniture, and his cooking utensils. The use of canvas screens afforded a certain amount of privacy whilst meals were eaten from a table shared with perhaps eight others.

In harbour, where discipline was relaxed, there was always a plentiful supply of food and drink. Meat was taken on board regularly, although for two days in each week it was replaced with sugar, cocoa and cheese. Some captains took several cows, goats and hens with them when they went to sea to supplement their rations, since officers and men alike received the same victuals, and if the cooks were far from expert, they nevertheless showed considerable ingenuity. They had to: the position of cook was one traditionally given to the wounded and so long as it afforded a man opportunity enough to make extra money, there was always competition for it.

Whilst officers provided their own cellars, wine was not officially permitted on the lower deck. It was always possible to obtain it, however: the women who came on board smuggled it in with them and the attempts made to halt the supply were rarely effective.

Efforts aimed at stemming the constant stream of women from coming on board were hardly successful either. As soon as a ship anchored in harbour, they were ferried out by bum-boat, in direct contravention of the regulations, and the normally cramped conditions became even worse. 'The whole of the shocking, disgraceful transactions of the lower deck it is impossible to describe,' petitioned Admiral Hawkins to the Admiralty as he tried to put an end to the practice, but there was really no satisfactory solution.

Some captains allowed only wives on board but understandably this only served to increase the traffic in forged marriage licences. Others evolved a scheme whereby only the best-behaved sailors were allowed feminine company, but such a plan was impossible to supervise and the women themselves were passed round from one man to another.

When it came to departure, some who were not permitted to remain eluded detection and remained throughout the voyage, sharing the rations and playing their own role in battle by helping the monkey-boys carry the powder from the magazines and nursing the wounded. Such women performed what was undeniably a valuable service but they were few and far between. The great majority of them, originally allowed on board as a form of reasonable indulgence, instead provoked only fights and arguments whilst constituting a serious hazard to health. The situation grew worse throughout the Napoleonic War and the problem was not finally solved until men were granted shore leave.

The mutiny at Spithead in 1797 was recognized for what it was—a justifiable protest against conditions in the Navy at the time. A sailor received no more pay in the 1790s than he did in the England of Oliver Cromwell, whereas the purchasing power of his money was less than half of what it was in the 1560s. In addition to their demands for a wage increase, the sailors demanded that less opportunity should be allowed for a certain few to make an illegal profit, that the sick should receive better treatment, that those wounded in action should continue to be paid until cured, and limited leave should be granted when in port.

The Admiralty put up a token resistance before acceding to what it admitted were reasonable claims, but a second mutiny broke out amongst the Nore ships which only harmed the seamen's cause. One by one, the crews involved deserted their leader, Richard Parker, and returned to the fold of authority. Parker himself was hanged, but the damage had been done; the second mutiny was both senseless and unnecessary and inevitably reflected badly on the Navy.

But if the life of a British sailor on the lower deck was being improved discipline and punishment was still harsh. The number of floggings on a receiving ship was particularly severe but, even on a man-of-war, the number of lashes inflicted for what amounted to only a minor offence, and for which the regulations stipulated should be no more than twelve, could be anything between three and six dozen.

Certainly there was room for considerably more improvement but by 1815, when Napoleon was finally defeated, a start had at least been made. Unfortunately, its progress was not to be maintained.

Ordinary Seaman, 1805

Captain of the Royal Marines in full-dress uniform, 1805

Royal Marine, 1805

CHAPTER SEVEN

The Ships

IT IS A fact that for the greater part of the Napoleonic War, the French Army enjoyed a success never once equalled by the French Navy. Whilst the Emperor himself and his marshals were able to subjugate one enemy after another on land, his admirals found it impossible to wrestle naval superiority from Britain. It was this failure which denied Napoleon the opportunity of invading England; it was this same failure which prompted his Continental System, and his efforts to enforce it led not only to his Peninsular campaign but also to his catastrophic invasion of Russia, which in turn resulted in his defeat at Leipzig in 1813 and his exile, short though it was, in Elba.

Napoleon was a product born of the French Revolution. Twenty years old at the time of the storming of the Bastille in 1789, the sweeping away of the privileged order of the aristocracy gave him the chance he needed and he lost no time in proving his military genius. He successfully repressed a royalist rising in Paris in 1795 and was given command of the French Army in Italy against the Austrians, winning victories at Lodi, Arcole and Rivioli in 1796 and 1797. Following the defeat of his fleet at the Battle of the Nile, he returned to France in 1799 and overthrew the Directory to establish his own dictatorship, defeating the Austrians at Marengo to break up the coalition which had been formed against France. Soon after the Treaty of Amiens in 1802, a plebiscite confirmed his consulship for life, and another in 1805 granted him the title of Emperor. A firm believer in the maxim that the end justified the means, he did not hesitate to deploy his troops for a frontal attack in which casualties were sure to be high. But at the same time, he inspired both love and confidence in his men; his generals, too, their origins often as humble as his own, commanded respect and obedience, and it was this devotion which helped give Napoleon the victories he both required and demanded.

His genius, however, did not extend to the sea. His Grand Design showed little understanding of nautical problems and confidence in his Navy was lacking. He did not trust his admirals, many of whom had aristocratic connexions, and there was resentment on the lower deck at the Emperor's obvious preoccupation with the military.

But if the French Army was superior on land, there was no doubt which Navy had control of the sea. England had a long tradition of naval supremacy; it was a supremacy which owed as much to the administrative ability of Hawkins in the sixteenth century and Pepys in the seventeenth as to the strategic cunning of the admirals, and in that the continuation of Britain's im-

The Emperor Napoleon Bonaparte (1769–1821). By Robert Lefèvre

portance as a world power relied heavily on her superiority at sea, such names as Rodney, Howe, Hood, St Vincent, Hawke and Nelson were worthy successors to Drake, Howard of Effingham, Raleigh and others.

Such men had long ago proved the advantage of manoeuvrability afloat; the ships which destroyed Philip of Spain's Armada of 1588 were far smaller than the top-heavy, lumbering hulks of the enemy, and the elimination of that manoeuvrability was an important factor in naval tactics in battle in the eighteenth century. So long as the masts and rigging remained intact, escape was always a possibility; destroy both and an exit ceased to exist.

Nelson's flagship at Trafalgar, HMS *Victory*, was built to the design of Sir Thomas Slade. Her keel was laid down at the Old Single Dock, Chatham, on July 23rd, 1759, but she was not launched until May 7th, 1765, and a further thirteen years were to pass before she was commissioned. She was always intended to be an admiral's flagship; the materials used were of the finest quality and, by the time she was completed, she was the most magnificent three-decked ship of the line of her day.

Preserved now in dry-dock in Portsmouth, her keel is just over 151 feet in length and 20 inches square, and her extreme breadth is 51 feet 10 inches. The ribs were fashioned from oak trees more than a hundred years old and, in all, 300,000 cubic feet of timber were needed for her construction. Her displacement is approximately 3,500 tons and she carried a crew of about 850 men.

Once she was launched, the lower masts were fixed to the keel and above them were added topmasts, topgallants and royals. It was at this stage in her construction that her captain and some of the crew first went on board. It was the responsibility of the master to ensure that all her sailing gear was in working order; the gunner arranged for the carriages to be swung into position before the guns themselves arrived from the ordnance factory. Shot and powder were delivered at the same time, as were muskets, cutlasses, pikes and other hand-weapons for distribution to the crew as and when the need arose. The boatswain's task was to supervise the rigging and the sails, and the carpenter had to familiarize himself with the structure of the ship, ready to carry out any repair which might be necessary. Only when all this was done, when the vessel was properly fitted out for sea, did the

HMS *Victory*, a drawing by G. H. Davis

captain set about finding his crew, and it was at this point in time that the pressgangs came into their own.

The *Victory* carried an armament of 102 guns, excluding two carronades which were positioned in the fo'c'sle. On the lower deck, there were thirty 32-pounders and two 12-pounders; on the middle deck, twenty-eight 24-pounders; on the upper deck, thirty 12-pounders; and on the quarterdeck, twelve 12-pounders. Her main magazine was situated well below the waterline where it could be flooded in the event of fire, and the overall length of the gun deck was 186 feet.

After Trafalgar, she was twice flagship in the Baltic and once off Spain. Her stern was altered in 1801 and further modifications were made to her bow between 1814 and 1816, but she has since been restored to her former condition at the time of Nelson's death.

The frigates played an important role in any action. It was their task to relay information from ship to ship, to give warning of an approaching enemy as well as to ensure that the fleet saw and understood the Commander-in-Chief's signals. Speed was essential and, in the twelve years between 1773 and 1785, about thirty were constructed for active service—an indication of the importance attached to them.

Four were present at Trafalgar: the *Euryalus,* commanded by Captain Blackwood; the *Naiad,* commanded by Captain Dundas; the *Phoebe,* commanded by Captain Capel; and the *Sirius,* commanded by Captain Prowse. Each averaged about 600 tons; their keels were almost 100 feet in length and the breadth of each vessel was about 34 feet. Armed with twenty-four 9-pounders with four smaller guns on the quarter deck, the gun deck itself was just over 120 feet long, and they each carried a crew of about 200 or so.

Inevitably there was a certain amount of confusion in the

fleets over the names of the ships. Some, particularly those of a classical nature, were common to all three Navies, and thus there was an English *Neptune*, a French *Neptune* and a Spanish *Neptuno*. The *Algéciras* was a French ship and not Spanish, as might be supposed; the *Berwick* was French and not English; and there was a French *Argonaute* and a Spanish *Argonauta*. The issue was further complicated by the fact that ships were more often captured than sunk and then reconditioned for service under new colours. The *Spartiate* and *Tonnant* were both originally French but having been captured at the Nile were now in the British Fleet, and often the same name was given to a new ship built by the original owners of the prize, which explains why there was a *Swiftsure* and *Achille* in both British and French Fleets.

The Carronade. Although primarily a naval gun, carronades were used extensively throughout the Napoleonic Wars and even formed part of the artillery at the Battle of Waterloo.

CHAPTER EIGHT

Aftermath

NEWS OF THE victory at Trafalgar was brought to England by Lieutenant Lapenotiere in the schooner *Pickle*, who landed at Falmouth on November 5th and reached London at half past one in the morning of the 6th. He went straightway to the Admiralty. Lord Barham was awoken with the news by William Marsden, the Secretary, and messages were sent to Nelson's brother, William, to his wife, and to Emma Hamilton at Merton, whilst copies of Collingwood's dispatch were made for the King, for Prime Minister Pitt, and for the *London Gazette*. (The effect on George III when he received his copy caused considerable consternation among the Court at Windsor: normally, the King hardly ever stopped talking; on this occasion, he was silent for almost five minutes.)

The dispatch itself, written on board the *Euryalus* (to which Collingwood had transferred his flag) off Cape Trafalgar on October 22nd, was published in *The Times* on November 7th. Collingwood began by giving a short account of the events leading up to the battle and then described the engagement itself:

'The action began at twelve o'clock, by the leading ships of the columns breaking through the enemy's line, the Commander in Chief about the tenth ship from the van, the Second in Command about the twelfth from the rear, leaving the van of the enemy unoccupied; the succeeding ships breaking through in all parts, astern of their leaders, and engaging the enemy at the muzzles of their guns; the conflict was severe; the enemy's ships were fought with a gallantry highly honourable to their Officers; but the attack on them was irresistible, and it pleased the Almighty Disposer of all events to grant his Majesty's arms a complete and glorious victory. About three P.M. many of the enemy's ships having struck their colours, their line gave way; Admiral Gravina, with ten ships joining their frigates to leeward, stood towards Cadiz. The five headmost ships in their van tacked, and standing to the Southward, to windward of the British line, were engaged, and the sternmost of them taken; the others went off, leaving to his Majesty's squadron nineteen ships of the line (of which two are first rates, the Santissima Trinidad and the Santa Anna,) with three Flag Officers, viz. Admiral Villeneuve, the Commander in Chief; Don Ignatio Maria D'Aliva, Vice Admiral; and the Spanish Rear-Admiral, Don Baltazar Hidalgo Cisneros.

'After such a Victory, it may appear unnecessary to enter into enconiums on the particular parts taken by the several Commanders; the conclusion says more on the subject than I have language to express; the spirit which animated all was the same:

when all exert themselves zealously in their country's service, all deserve that their high merit should stand recorded; and never was high merit more conspicuous than in the battle I have described.'

Collingwood then continued on a more personal note:

'Such a battle could not be fought without sustaining a great loss of men. I have not only to lament, in common with the British Navy, and the British Nation, in the Fall of the Commander in Chief, the loss of a Hero, whose name will be immortal, and his memory ever dear to his country; but my heart is rent with the most poignant grief for the death of a friend, to whom, by many years intimacy, and a perfect knowledge of the virtues of his mind, which supplied ideas superior to the common race of men, I was bound by the strongest ties of affection, a grief to which even the glorious occasion in which he fell, does not bring the consolation which, perhaps, it ought. . . .'

Collingwood's words were echoed throughout the country. This time there was little rejoicing, the sense of loss at Nelson's death overclouding the glory of the victory. Indeed, Lord Malmesbury wrote that 'every common person in the streets [is] speaking first of their sorrow for Nelson, and then of the victory'.

The task of preserving Nelson's body fell to the *Victory's* surgeon, Dr Beatty, and he placed the remains in a cask of spirits. The wounded were disembarked at Gibraltar on October 28th and one week later, the *Victory* sailed back through the Straits to rejoin Collingwood before making her way home, through heavy seas, to England.

On December 23rd, in the Nore, Nelson's coffin was taken on board the Admiralty Commissioners' yacht and carried to Greenwich, where the body was to lie in state. Some thirty thousand people filed sadly past, and on January 8th, in a severe gale and attended by nine admirals, five hundred Greenwich pensioners and the Lord Mayor and Corporation of London, Nelson embarked on his last journey. The coffin, made of wood from the *L'Orient* which had fought at the Battle of the Nile, was taken up-river to the Admiralty and from there, at eight-thirty the following morning, preceded by the Scots Greys and immediately followed by thirty flag officers and a hundred captains, to St Paul's Cathedral, where it was lowered by twelve

Sir William Beatty (1773?–1842), wearing Physician's full-dress uniform (1805–25). By A. W. Devis (1763–1822)

Nelson's Flagships, a commemorative painting by Nicholas Pocock (1741–1821). Nelson's favourite ship, the *Agamemnon*, 64, is on the extreme left; broadside on is the *Vanguard*, 74, his flagship at the Nile, and stern on is the *Elephant*, his temporary flagship at Copenhagen. The *Victory* is on the right, and beyond her is the *Captain*, 74, in which he flew a Commodore's broad pendant at St Vincent

Emma, Lady Hamilton (1761?–1815), a pastel by J. Schmidt, dated 1800, which Nelson referred to as his 'Guardian Angel'

sailors from the *Victory* into the black and white sarcophagus which had originally been made for Cardinal Wolsey.

Nelson was succeeded to the peerage, which was raised to an earldom, by his brother William, a clergyman of whom Collingwood opined: 'Of all the dull stupid fellows you ever saw, perhaps he is the most so. . . . Fortune, in one of her frisks, raised him, without his body and mind having anything to do with it, to the highest dignity.' Parliament awarded him a grant of £90,000 in addition to an annual pension, 'for ever', of £5,000. (In fact, Parliament decided the pension should cease just after the Second World War.) Nelson's sisters were each granted £15,000, and for his widow, Fanny, who died in 1831, there was an annuity of £2,000.

In spite of the codicil which Nelson had made to his will on the morning of the battle, however, Emma Hamilton and his daughter, Horatia, received nothing. 'I leave Emma Lady Hamilton, therefore,' Nelson had written, 'a Legacy to my King and Country, that they will give her an ample provision to maintain her Rank of Life. I also leave to the beneficence of my Country my adopted daughter, Horatia Nelson Thompson [sic]; and I desire she will use in future the name of Nelson only. These are the only favours I ask my King and Country at this moment when I am going to fight their Battle.'

Instead, they were ignored. Emma, however, was well provided for both by Nelson and her late husband, Sir William Hamilton, but through her own extravagance and recklessness she died penniless in Calais in 1815. Horatia was adopted by Nelson's younger sister and eventually married the Reverend Philip Ward, living on until 1881.

Collingwood was created a baron and given a pension of £2,000 a year for life, although if he was survived by his widow, she would receive £1,000 and his daughters £500. That he had no son meant that the title became extinct upon his death and his requests to allow it to descend through the female line were disregarded.

Sir Richard Strachan was promoted Rear-Admiral and awarded the Order of the Bath for his capture of Dumanoir le Pelley, and he also received an annuity of £1,000.

Lord Barham, the architect of the Trafalgar campaign, was

allowed to retire for the second time, living on in the country until his death in his eighty-seventh year in 1813.

The Battle of Trafalgar marked both the beginning and the end of an epoch: the beginning of more than a hundred years of undisputed British naval supremacy, and the end of the large-scale battles fought under sail. But the campaign itself was essentially an offensive one and the action off Cape Trafalgar was fought with the object of annihilating the French Fleet and thereby putting an end to Napoleon's threats of invasion whilst confirming Britain's superiority afloat. In that it was supremely successful. It stands out as one of Britain's greatest moments, a victory nourished and preserved by legend which persists even to this day. Nelson's flagship, the *Victory*, is now in drydock in Portsmouth; Trafalgar Square in London is one of the landmarks of the capital; the National Maritime Museum at Greenwich houses Nelson's relics. All these ensure that the battle fought on October 21st, 1805, at which England's greatest naval hero lost his life, will never be forgotten.

Horatio, Viscount Nelson, Vice-Admiral of the White. By an unknown sculptor

The British Fleet:

WEATHER COLUMN

(Twelve ships of the line under the command of Vice-Admiral Viscount Nelson, KB, Duke of Bronte)

Victory (flagship), 104 guns: Vice-Admiral Horatio Nelson, Captain Thomas Masterman Hardy
57 killed, 75 wounded
Téméraire, 98 guns: Captain Eliab Harvey
47 killed, 76 wounded
Neptune, 98 guns: Captain Thomas Francis Fremantle
10 killed, 34 wounded
Leviathan, 74 guns: Captain Henry William Bayntun
4 killed, 22 wounded
Conqueror, 74 guns: Captain Israel Pellew
3 killed, 9 wounded

Britannia, 100 guns: Rear-Admiral the Earl of Northesk, Captain Charles Bullen
10 killed, 40 wounded
Ajax, 74 guns: Lieutenant John Pilford
2 killed, 2 wounded
Agamemnon, 64 guns: Captain Sir Edward Berry
2 killed, 7 wounded
Orion, 74 guns: Captain Edward Codrington
1 killed, 21 wounded
Minotaur, 74 guns: Captain Charles John Moore Mansfield
3 killed, 20 wounded
Spartiate, 74 guns: Captain Sir Francis Laforey, Bart
3 killed, 17 wounded
Africa, 64 guns: Captain Henry Digby
18 killed, 37 wounded

The British Fleet:

LEE COLUMN

(Fifteen ships of the line under the command of Vice-Admiral Cuthbert Collingwood)

Royal Sovereign, 100 guns: Vice-Admiral Cuthbert Collingwood, Captain Edward Rotherham
47 killed, 94 wounded

Belleisle, 74 guns: Captain William Hargood
33 killed, 93 wounded

Mars, 74 guns: Captain George Duff
29 killed, 69 wounded

Tonnant, 80 guns: Captain Charles Tyler
26 killed, 50 wounded

Bellerophon, 74 guns: Captain John Cooke
27 killed, 123 wounded

Colossus, 74 guns: Captain James Nicoll Morris
43 killed, 110 wounded

Achille, 74 guns: Captain Richard King
13 killed, 59 wounded

Revenge, 74 guns: Captain Robert Moorsom
28 killed, 51 wounded

Defiance, 74 guns: Captain Philip Charles Durham
17 killed, 53 wounded

Swiftsure, 74 guns: Captain William George Rutherford
9 killed, 8 wounded

Dreadnought, 98 guns: Captain John Conn
7 killed, 26 wounded

Polythemus, 64 guns: Captain Richard Redmill
2 killed, 4 wounded

Prince, 98 guns: Captain Richard Grindall
0 killed, 0 wounded

Thunderer, 74 guns: Lieutenant John Stockham
4 killed, 12 wounded

Defence, 74 guns: Captain George Hope
7 killed, 29 wounded

Additional ships present:

Frigate *Euryalus*: Captain the Honourable Henry Blackwood
Frigate *Naiad*: Captain Thomas Dundas
Frigate *Phoebe*: Captain the Honourable Thomas Bladen Capel
Frigate *Sirius*: Captain William Prowse
Schooner *Pickle*: Lieutenant John Richards Lapenotiere
Cutter *Entreprenante*: Lieutenant R. B. Young

The Combined Franco-Spanish Fleet:

THE FRENCH FLEET

(Eighteen ships of the line under the command of Vice-Admiral Pierre Villeneuve)

Scipion, 74 guns: Captain Charles Berenger
  17 killed, 22 wounded
Intrépide, 74 guns: Commodore Louis Antoine Cyprian Infernet
  half of crew killed
Formidable, 80 guns: Rear-Admiral P. R. M. E. Dumanoir le Pelley, Captain Jean Marie Letellier
  22 killed, 45 wounded
Mont-Blanc, 74 guns: Commodore G. J. Noel la Villegris
  20 killed, 24 wounded
Duguay-Trouin, 74 guns: Captain Claude Touffet
  12 killed, 24 wounded
Heros, 74 guns: Captain Jean B. J. Remi Poulain
  12 killed, 26 wounded
Bucentaure (flagship), 80 guns: Vice-Admiral Pierre Charles Jean Baptiste Silvestre Villeneuve, Captain Jean Jacques Magendie
  197 killed, 85 wounded
Redoutable, 74 guns: Captain Jean Jacques Étienne Lucas
  490 killed, 81 wounded
Neptune, 80 guns: Commodore Esprit Tranquille Maistral
  15 killed, 39 wounded

Indomptable, 80 guns: Commodore Jean Joseph Hubert
  two-thirds of crew drowned
Fougueux, 74 guns: Captain Louis Baudoin
  546 casualties
Pluton, 74 guns: Commodore Julien Cosmao
  60 killed, 132 wounded
Algéciras, 74 guns: Rear-Admiral Charles Magon, Captain Gabriel Auguste Brouard
  77 killed, 143 wounded
Aigle, 74 guns: Captain Pierre Paul Gourrège
  two-thirds of crew killed
Swiftsure, 74 guns: Captain C. E. L'Hospitalier Villemadrin
  68 killed, 123 wounded
Argonaute, 74 guns: Captain Jacques Epron
  55 killed, 137 wounded
Achille, 74 guns: Captain Gabriel de Nieport
  480 casualties
Berwick, 74 guns: Captain Jean Gilles Filhol Camas
  entire crew drowned

Additional ships present:

Frigates *Cornelie, Hermione, Hortense, Rhin, Thémis*
Brigantines *Argus, Furet*

The Combined Franco-Spanish Fleet:

THE SPANISH FLEET

(Fifteen ships of the line under the command of Admiral Don Federico Gravina)

Neptuno, 80 guns: Commodore Don Cayetano Valdès
    38 killed, 35 wounded
Rayo, 100 guns: Commodore Don Enrique Macdonell
    4 killed, 14 wounded
San Francisco de Asis, 74 guns: Captain Don Luis de Flores
    5 killed, 12 wounded
San Augustin, 74 guns: Captain Don Felipe Xado Cagigal
    184 killed, 201 wounded
Santissima Trinidad, 130 guns: Rear-Admiral Don B. Hidalgo Cisneros, Commodore Don Francisco de Uriarte
    216 killed, 116 wounded
San Justo, 74 guns: Captain Don Miguel Gaston
    0 killed, 7 wounded
San Leandro, 64 guns: Captain Don Josef Quevedo
    8 killed, 22 wounded

Santa Ana, 112 guns: Vice-Admiral Don Ignatius Maria D'Alava, Captain Don Josef Guardoqui
    104 killed, 137 wounded
Monarca, 74 guns: Captain Don Teodoro Argumosa
    101 killed, 154 wounded
Bahama, 74 guns: Captain Don Dionisio Galiano
    75 killed, 66 wounded
Montanez, 74 guns: Captain Don Josef Salcedo
    20 killed, 29 wounded
San Ildefonso, 74 guns: Captain Don Josef Bargas
    36 killed, 124 wounded
Argonauta, 80 guns: Commodore Don Antonio Pareja
    103 killed, 202 wounded
Principe de Asturias (flagship), 112 guns: Admiral Don Federico Gravina, Rear-Admiral Don Antonio Escano
    54 killed, 109 wounded
San Juan de Nepomuceno, 74 guns: Captain Don Cosme Churruca
    103 killed, 131 wounded

Comparative Casualty Figures:

	killed	wounded
THE BRITISH FLEET		
Weather Column:	160	360
Lee Column:	294	781
Total:	454	1,141

	killed	wounded
THE COMBINED FRANCO–SPANISH FLEET		
The French Fleet:	1,035★	1,359★
The Spanish Fleet:	1,051	861
Total:	2,086★	2,220★
Cumulative Total:	2,540★	3,361

★ These figures exclude those casualties on board the French ships *Indomptable*, *Intrépide*, *Aigle*, *Berwick*, *Achille* and *Fougueux*, for which it has not been possible to obtain exact details.

Comparative Numbers of Ships of the Line:

THE BRITISH FLEET
Weather Column: 12
Lee Column: 15
                                                   ——
Total: 27
                                                   ——

THE COMBINED FRANCO–SPANISH FLEET
The French Fleet: 18
The Spanish Fleet: 15
                                                   ——
Total: 33
                                                   ——

Cumulative Total: ——
                                                   60
                                                   ——

Comparative Gun Strengths of Ships of the Line:

THE BRITISH FLEET

Weather Column:	972
Lee Column:	1,116
Total:	2,088

THE COMBINED FRANCO–SPANISH FLEET

The French Fleet:	1,356
The Spanish Fleet:	1,470
Total:	2,826
Cumulative Total:	4,914

64

H.M.S. *Victory* as she can be seen today, in dry-dock in Portsmouth.